LEAD

THE

FIELD

LEAD
THE
FIELD

HOW TO

BECOME AN AUTHORITY AND
DOMINATE YOUR COMPETITION

ADAM D. WITTY

Advantage®

Published by Advantage, Charleston, South Carolina.
Member of Advantage Media Group.

ADVANTAGE is a registered trademark and the Advantage colophon is a trademark of Advantage Media Group, Inc.

Printed in the United States of America.

ISBN: 978-1-59932-747-1
LCCN: 2016900361

This publication is designed to provide accurate and authoritative information in regard to the subject matter covered. It is sold with the understanding that the publisher is not engaged in rendering legal, accounting, or other professional services. If legal advice or other expert assistance is required, the services of a competent professional person should be sought.

Advantage Media Group is proud to be a part of the Tree Neutral® program. Tree Neutral offsets the number of trees consumed in the production and printing of this book by taking proactive steps such as planting trees in direct proportion to the number of trees used to print books. To learn more about Tree Neutral, please visit www.treeneutral.com. To learn more about Advantage's commitment to being a responsible steward of the environment, please visit www.advantagefamily.com/green

Advantage Media Group is a publisher of business, self-improvement, and professional development books and online learning. We help entrepreneurs, business leaders, and professionals share their Stories, Passion, and Knowledge to help others Learn & Grow™. Do you have a manuscript or book idea that you would like us to consider for publishing? Please visit advantagefamily.com or call 1.866.775.1696.

This book is dedicated to the entrepreneurs, business leaders, and professionals that have Stories, Passion, and Knowledge to share with the world.

TABLE OF CONTENTS

THE POWER OF AUTHORITY

by Dan Kennedy

America's #1 Marketing Advisor,
author of over 20 best-selling marketing books

dankennedy.com
nobsbooks.com

There is a huge secret about income that only a small percentage of top earners in every field ever figure out and use to their advantage. Most others are ignorant of it, but some see it, and instead of using it, they deeply and bitterly resent it. The secret is that *the higher up in income you go, in almost any category, the more you are paid for who you are rather than for what you do*. That often isn't just, in the way that most people think about justice, and I can't attempt to affect how you think about this in the few words I have for the introduction to this book, so for now I'll simply state it as the bald fact that it is.

The number-one key to making yourself a powerful, magnetic, trusted, high-income "who" to any target audience or market is your known and accepted status as an authority.

BE SEEN AS THE AUTHORITY, NOT THE SALESPERSON

If you are wandering about in the forest, you will probably recognize a bear if you encounter one. You know bears are big, furry, black or brown, with snouts, and so on. You've seen photos. You've seen them on TV and in movies.

Similarly, you know how to spot a dreaded salesperson in the woods. He has lots of brochures, maybe a PowerPoint presentation on a laptop, and other sales matter. He usually assaults you and tries to get you to an appointment by various stratagems. In his cubicle or office, there are plaques and trophies proclaiming his sales prowess. Like bears, these sales creatures are to be feared and avoided.

Although I have been a salesman virtually every day of my life, I have gone to great pains not to be perceived as one. Beginning very early in my career to the present, I have implemented an overall marketing strategy to elevate my authority in the minds of my clientele so that I am not perceived as a salesman. Rather, my business comes to me because *money follows and flows to authority.*

For me, the journey toward this authority status began when I first published *The Ultimate Sales Letter* in 1981—a book that has been on bookstore shelves without interruption ever since. It established me as an expert in the craftsmanship of letters that sell. It directly brought me clients, but much more importantly, it elevated my status above other copywriters. People wanted to hear from and get assistance from "the guy who wrote the book" about sales letters, and it is not accidental that the preemptive word "the" is in that title.

I have since written more than thirty books with seven different publishing companies and have gone to considerable effort to effectively implement an ongoing marketing strategy around them, keeping them in print and distribution and using the authority conveyed by being the author of each book and of an entire series of books to every possible advantage.

Back when I flew commercial—I now travel by private jet—and when I was still on the hunt for clients and business, I always had copies of my books in my carry-on. In 1985, I was in first-class, on a flight from Phoenix to Houston, and the fellow next to me struck up the usual conversation. He identified himself as owner of a Houston-based advertising agency and asked what I did. Instead of an answer or "elevator speech," I stood up, got a copy of *The Ultimate Sales Letter* book, handed it to him, and excused myself for a trip to the bathroom. Two weeks later, I was conducting a nicely compensated training session for his staff copywriters, where he proudly told them, "Today, I have brought you the man who wrote the book on sales letter writing."

One more story about that first book: the owner of a very large, fast-growing weight-loss company with a hot celebrity endorser, a robust direct-marketing campaign, and distribution in Wal-Mart brought me to his company headquarters to spend a day discussing direct marketing with his entire staff, followed by a second day working with his three copywriters.

At the start of the first day, he told me he had given *The Ultimate Sales Letter* to everybody a week before so that they would be prepared. He then asked if everybody had read it and announced he was going to conduct a quick, impromptu quiz on the book before I got started. One guy sheepishly admitted he'd been too busy to read the book. My client instantly fired him.

He said, "I've invested in bringing the number-one expert in this field in. If you couldn't invest an hour or two preparing, I do not wish to continue investing in you."

Clients acquire status by having a leading expert working for them. Typically, when prospective clients come to me as a referral, they report that the referring client either told them about one of my books and urged them to get it and read it or gifted them one of my books.

This is what I call the "expert status halo." People are proud of their association with an expert, be that the number-one expert on home decorating in Abilene or the number-one expert on direct-response marketing and copywriting in the world (me).

MUST YOU SELL OR CAN YOU PRESCRIBE?

Certain experts, professionals, and providers do not sell their recommendations; they have the authority needed to prescribe.

Authority comes from a matrix of factors, including expert status as well as environment, mind-set of customer, criticality of solution, and others. If you have a stomachache that won't go away and hustle over to the local "doc-in-a-box" urgent-care clinic, you'll probably fill a prescription he issues without question, but you probably wouldn't let him cut you open and remove an organ without a lot of questions; you would demand a second opinion.

However, if your chronic stomach pain takes you from your MD to a specialist at the Cleveland Clinic, who brings in another specialist, and they prescribe urgent surgery, you most likely will sign the form, lie down on the steel cart, and be wheeled away without checking out information via Google.

The solution proposed is the same in both scenarios. *The difference in your reaction is entirely based on your acceptance of the authority of the person making the recommendation.*

In my own consulting and copywriting practice, I often present complex projects that involve fees from $75,000 to $200,000, plus royalties, and are often more complex and require more investment than a new client has prepared himself for. I never want to have to sell such a thing. I have developed a thorough, carefully choreographed process to avoid having to sell my service.

The following is a brief overview: A potential client typically comes forward from my books, from a referral, from participating in a seminar, or from within Glazer-Kennedy Insider's Circle (GKIC) membership. The potential client is prevented from contacting me via phone or otherwise and instead is required to fax me a memo describing his business and perceived needs. He first receives a written reply, usually accompanied by one or several of my books. He must then take the initiative to book a consulting day, positioned as "diagnostic and prescriptive" (at my base fee of $18,800).

He may be told of or sent a book of mine to read. He has to travel to me for the day. Before day's end, he is asking me to issue a prescription—which I do. And nine out of ten times it is accepted. This is the power of authority.

Great GKIC members in a very different field, Jeff Giagnocavo and Ben McClure, are authors of *What's Keeping You Up at Night?* and owners of Gardner's Mattress, where their mattresses are priced from $4,000 to $35,000, even while encircled by mattress stores selling at or below the national average of $700.

I am impressed by and very proud of these guys. Everybody else sells mattresses. They prescribe.

In the store, the customer is engaged in a diagnostic conversation. For many, a particular mattress is then prescribed and taken from the showroom floor into the private Dream Room®, a room that mimics a luxury hotel suite, where the customer and spouse spend one, two, or even three hours—

they are able to nap, watch TV, read, and fully, comfortably experience the chosen bed.

To date, the percentage of customers who buy after trying out the bed in the Dream Room® is—drum roll, please—100 percent.

This is the power of authority.

One of the GKIC members in my top coaching program is Steve Adams, the owner of twenty-one exceptionally profitable retail pet stores. In each store, there is a professional pet nutrition counselor who engages customers in a diagnostic process to then prescribe the best customized diet and food for that person's pet. The total customer value and retention is much, much higher than ordinary stores manage.

That's the power of authority.

If you want to be liberated from selling, if you want to prescribe rather than sell, then you need to focus on building your status, building your authority, and becoming the leader in your field.

THE IRRATIONAL REACTION
TO STAR POWER

As I am writing this, there are two supremely suc-cessful TV ad campaigns you have probably seen *ad nauseam*: one for an herbal prostate remedy, starring former NFL quarterback Joe Theisman, the other for investing in gold, starring the gray-haired, rugged-looking actor William Devane.

These campaigns are minting money with star power because people react irrationally to celebri-ties and celebrity endorsements. And at all levels, NetJets's sales improved as soon as Warren Buf-fett bought the company. Warren is a rich person's celebrity. He is not an expert in air travel safety. Levitra® was made popular beginning with ads starring former Chicago Bears coach Mike Ditka, a cigar-chomping tough guy—a man's man, but not an expert on medicine.

If people were rational, it would be better to promote NetJets with a highly credentialed expert in aircraft maintenance and to promote Levitra® with a top doctor from the Harvard Medical School.

I have used star power by association, rented star power, and manufactured star power throughout my business life, with celebrity endorsements from the likes of Joan Rivers and Fox Business economics expert Harry Dent. Top celebrity speakers such as Brian Tracy and Tom Hopkins have written introductions to books for me, and I even got an endorsement from a contestant on Donald Trump's TV show *The Apprentice* in which she says, "Even Donald Trump could learn a thing or two from Dan's book."

My authority status is what draws 1,000 to 1,500 entrepreneurs to our major GKIC events, and I welcome those that buy six, eight, or twenty books to be autographed and given to friends because they're working as a subtle sales force, reaching lots of people I might never reach otherwise, at no out-of-pocket cost, bringing new customers to GKIC and occasionally a client to me.

This authority status also draws others to me, who want to be associated with me through endorsements or even co-authorship of a book because this allows them to position themselves further in their own fields as experts and authorities.

I have also gotten a lot of speaking engagements on programs where I've appeared—often repeatedly—with an eclectic collection of political, business, and world leaders and Hollywood and sports celebrities. I've spent nine years with the famous SUCCESS events (held in sports arenas with audiences of 10,000 to 35,000), and I've attended many clients' events.

I often urge clients to hire celebrity speakers; at GKIC events, where we always use at least one celebrity entrepreneur, the list has included Gene

Simmons (KISS), Joan Rivers, Ivanka Trump, John Rich (winner, *Celebrity Apprentice*) and Barbara Corcoran (*Shark Tank*).

Because of my plan, I have been able to work with a lot of impressive people whose names should arguably not influence others' thinking about my value as an advisor on business or marketing matters. There is no rational link between my appearing on programs with these people and my expertise and trustworthiness as someone to tell you how to invest your money in advertising and marketing.

It should not be influential. But it is.

Partial List Of Celebrities, Authors, Business Leaders & Others Dan Kennedy Has Appeared On Programs With As A Speaker

Political & World Leaders
President Gerald Ford*
President Ronald Reagan*
President George Bush*
Gen. Norman Schwarzkopf*
Secretary Colin Powell*
Mikail Gorbachev*
Lady Margaret Thatcher*
William Bennett*

Legendary Entrepreneurs
Mark McCormack* *Sports Agent, Founder IMG, Author, What They Don't Teach You At Harvard Business School)*
Ben & Jerry*
(Ben & Jerry's Ice Cream)
Debbi Fields*
(Mrs. Fields Cookies)
Jim McCann*
(1-800-Flowers)
Joe Sugarman*
(Blu-Blockers)
Donald Trump

Hollywood Personalities & Entertainers
Bill Cosby*
Johnny Cash
Naomi Judd*
Mary Tyler Moore*
Christopher Reeve*
The Smothers Brothers
Willard Scott*
Barbara Walters
Charlton Heston

Broadcasters
Larry King*
Paul Harvey*
Deborah Norville

Authors & Speakers
Zig Ziglar* *(See You At The Top)*
Brian Tracy*
Jim Rohn*
Tom Hopkins*
Mark Victor Hansen*
(Chicken Soup For The Soul)
Tony Robbins* *(Unlimited Power)*
Mike Vance* *(Dean, Disney Univ.; Think Outside The Box)*
Michael Gerber *(E-Myth)*

Sports Personalities, Athletes & Coaches
Joe Montana*
Troy Aikman*
Peyton Manning*
Mike Singletarry
Coach Tom Landry*
Coach Jimmy Johnson*
Coach Lou Holtz*
Dick Vitale*
George Foreman*
Muhammad Ali*
Mary Lou Retton*
Bonnie Blair*
Dan Jansen

Other Newsmakers
Lt. Col. Oliver North
Gerry Spence*
Alan Dershowitz*
Capt. Scott O'Grady*

Health
Dr. Ted Broer*
Dr. Jack Groppel*

AUTHORITY MARKETING: THE TRIFECTA OF MAGNETIC ATTRACTION AND RISING INCOME

If you wish to achieve fame and status in your field, you must design and implement an Authority Marketing plan that includes multiple strategies—including book authorship—to position yourself as an undisputed expert, influential authority, and in-demand celebrity.

When you combine expert status, authority, and celebrity, you cash in a winning trifecta ticket. These three factors, working in concert, act to deliver three very desirable benefits: you are made able to more readily attract more and better clients/customers, make selling to them easier, and make price less of an issue so that the profitability of your business improves.

How do you achieve that trifecta most effectively and efficiently? With the power of Authority Marketing.

WHY SHOULD ANYONE LISTEN TO YOU?

I t's a fair question. What about you stands out from the crowd in your chosen profession? Why should anyone purchase your product or service, listen to your opinion over someone else in the same field, or search you out specifically for these things?

Because you are *the* authority.

Because prospective clients trust you more than your competition and because you know more than the other guys. Because you've established yourself as the leading authority in your field, and you have gone to great lengths to ensure that this is known to every one of your potential clients.

That is the power of Authority Marketing.

When I started Advantage Media Group as a publishing house over ten years ago, I really thought that I was in the book-selling business. And at first, I was. But what I realized over time is that I'm not in the book business; I'm really in the marketing business. And I'm not just in the marketing business; I'm in the Authority Marketing business.

Because establishing yourself as *the* authority, the thought leader, and the expert in your field is ultimately how you're able to command outsize influence over others and to dominate your competition.

Why should anyone listen to you? Because you are the authority on the subject, and in many cases, you "wrote the book" on the subject.

Becoming an authority in your field and in your community allows you to create an *unfair advantage* in the marketplace by immediately positioning you above others in the same field, and it *opens doors*, which, in the end, is the single most important responsibility of any business owner/ CEO: to acquire and retain customers.

This book is not about writing and publishing a book. Yes, to solidify your place as an authority on any topic, authoring a book on the subject is often a mandatory step, but becoming the authority requires a more robust and strategic plan.

There are twenty-eight million businesses in America, but fewer than 4 percent ever surpass $1 million in annual revenue, while fewer than 0.4 percent ever surpass $10 million in annual revenue. Only 17,000 ever surpass $50 million in annual revenue. Why? Because they never get their marketing puzzle figured out.

Many CEOs fail to realize the fact that people buy relationships, not corporations. Buying is an emotional experience, and the most enlightened CEOs know that people buy emotionally and then justify their purchase with logic. The greater the connection CEOs foster between potential clients and a center of influence—those who can boost their market access and credibility through referrals and testimonials—the better chance they have to gain a customer for their business.

Positioning yourself and your business as *the* authority is the cornerstone of generating that emotional connection.

Are you ready to push your business past the $1 million, $10 million, or $50 million wall? Are you ready to stand out in your field and become the authority in your industry? Are you ready to open more doors with prospects and clients than you ever imagined? Then read on and discover how Authority Marketing is the key to unlocking these opportunities and more.

CHAPTER 1

BREAKING THROUGH THE BRICK WALL

f you're reading this book, you already understand the importance and value of building authority in your field.

Of the twenty-eight million businesses in the United States, those that surpass the $10 million and $50 million annual revenue milestones make it because they're focused singularly on one goal: hypergrowth. That is, the more doors they open, the more clients they will attract.

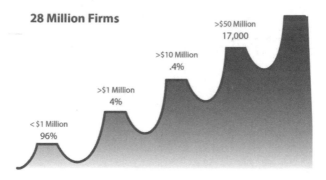

28 Million Firms

>$50 Million
17,000

>$10 Million
.4%

>$1 Million
4%

< $1 Million
96%

How do these companies achieve hypergrowth? How do they open those doors and keep opening them effectively?

By creating authority in their field and leveraging that authority to give them as many unfair advantages over their competition as possible.

THE VALUE OF UNFAIR ADVANTAGES

By definition, an unfair advantage is "a unique way of organizing your thinking, communication, and action in more productive ways that competitors can neither comprehend nor copy."

The greatest entrepreneurs and CEOs are those who have created the largest number of unfair advantages for themselves. Take Herb Kellcher, cofounder of Southwest Airlines, who created a massive number of unfair advantages when he decided to fly point-to-point, turn a plane in twenty minutes, offer no assigned seats, serve no meals, and fly only one model of airplane. Forty years later, the other major airlines still haven't caught up!

On perhaps a more relatable level, consider the criminal defense law firm of John Patrick Dolan in Southern California.

If you open the phone book in SoCal, you'll find more than a hundred other firms competing with John within a fifty-mile radius. John created an unfair advantage for himself when he wrote the book *Negotiate Like the Pros*. This book established John as the number-one authority on negotiation, a trait that is important to most people who are in need of a criminal defense attorney. Then he sprinkled MiracleGro on this unfair advantage when he marketed that book, getting copies to producers at CNN, MSNBC, and Fox News. He began appearing on major cable television almost weekly as a "legal commentator and author of *Negotiate Like the Pros*."

John's phone rings off the hook. His firm cherry-picks the cases they want and pass on the rest. By creating the unfair advantage of authority for himself and leveraging it with a deliberately implemented marketing plan, John dramatically differentiated himself from every other criminal defense attorney.

AUTHORITY CAN BE MANUFACTURED

What every entrepreneur and CEO should understand is that authority does not happen blindly. It does not happen will-lessly. It does not creep up on you in the darkness of night. It happens over time, and it is deliberately created. Some methods for creating authority are through the establishment of past achievements, awards, professional designation, and experience.

Of course, you may spend half a lifetime building this line of authority for yourself when out of the blue, another person in your profession with less than half of your experience may skyrocket past you in authority ranking.

This "Super Authority" may seem sudden to others, but it's the product of deliberate actions, of positioning yourself in a broad range of effective marketing campaigns (see more on these in Chapter 5: The Seven Pillars of Authority Marketing), and using unfair advantages to outflank and distance yourself from the competition.

Simply put, authority can be—and often is—manufactured.

AUTHORITY TO BUILD TRUST

Advantage authors Matt Zagula and Dan Kennedy authored a book a few years back titled *How to Create Trust in an Understandably Untrustworthy World*. Trust, while the most important part of making a sale, is also the most difficult to achieve, and by positioning yourself and your company as trustworthy—and specifically more trustworthy than your competition—you win business and feed into the acceleration of your company's hypergrowth.

Trust, according to Matt and Dan, can be built on a number of factors, each of which is a valuable component of an effective Authority Marketing plan because trust, to clients, is essentially interchangeable with authority.

Take Dan's examples of Joe Theisman and William Devane in the Foreword section on "The Irrational Reaction to Star Power." In Dan's own words, these icons "are minting money with star power because people react irrationally to celebrities and celebrity endorsements."

People see the status of being well-known as a basis for trust. Therefore, if you're well-known as an expert in your field, then you've established that first essential connection with your clients.

In order to build trust, however, you must be "out there" on multiple levels, not just with a book but through campaigns embracing every type of media, including word-of-mouth, to the point where if someone in your target market hasn't heard of you, they've almost certainly been living without contact from the outside world for far too long.

I go into several of the most valuable components of an effective Authority Marketing strategy in Chapter 5: The Seven Pillars of Authority Marketing, but briefly, establishing that trust/authority in your field requires a solid marketing campaign focusing on all aspects of media consumption, from blogging to radio shows to press releases and event hosting.

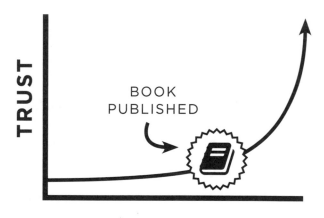

It may seem like a hell of a hurdle at first, but keep in mind that an effective marketing campaign is not implemented in one full-on attack but rather over time, building on each smaller success to achieve greater ones until it almost becomes a self-perpetuating cycle.

By building on this essential value of trust and accelerating your trust value through the development and growth of you and your business's authority, you can double, triple, and even quadruple the response rate of prospects compared to nonauthority marketing tactics.

And the more trust you gain, the more likely it is that potential clients will purposefully seek you out and so on, propelling your business into that all-too-coveted position of hypergrowth.

CHAPTER 2

CLIENTS SHOULD COME TO YOU, NOT THE OTHER WAY AROUND

I f you've ever been offshore fishing for blue marlin, you know that this six-hundred-plus-pound behemoth is one of the most difficult saltwater fish to catch in the world. Landing one requires tremendous skill and just the right bait.

Now, if I were to offer you two options for catching blue marlin—a fishing net or a precisely tuned outrigger-led fishing line with just the right blue marlin bait or lure—which would you take?

It seems like an obvious answer, but when you relate it to hypergrowing your business, it's amazing how many people choose to go with the net when it comes to marketing and building their authority. Instead of putting something out there that their exact target market is desperate to have (or giving the impression that they *absolutely have to have it*), they instead take a big old net and sling it as best they can into the water, hoping to draw up something good.

To further the analogy, throwing a big, heavy, soaking wet net into the ocean time and again can wear you out quickly, whereas sitting patiently with a line is a more strategic process. Then, when the prospective fish is snagged, you put everything you have into it because you know that the exact fish you want is on the other end of that line.

So why are you wearing out your arms throwing a net over and over again into murky water? Why aren't you developing just the right bait and strategically positioning yourself so that your target audience comes to you?

THE MAGNET PRINCIPLE

If you're attracting your target customer, turning yourself into a magnet instead of casting around for whatever's about, then you will ultimately attract better people and better opportunities to you and your business.

This principle goes beyond the client, as well. To hypergrow your business, you need to attract far more than just your target audience. You also need to attract all-star employees to help you build that relationship and develop the invaluable trust needed to grow and retain your customer base, and you need to attract publicity, media, and speaking opportunities to continue building your authority.

Are desirable employees and opportunities attracted to you? Do clients come to you instead of the other way around? Can you command the way you do business without your customers blinking an eye because they trust you implicitly? If not, then you need to drop the net and start learning how to fish.

CHAPTER 3

THE POWER
OF AUTHORITY
MARKETING

By definition, Authority Marketing is the **strategic process** of **systematically positioning** a person or an organization as the leader and expert in their industry, community, and marketplace to **command outsize influence over all competitors.**

There are a few key terms here, which I've highlighted in the definition. The first is "strategic process."

Strategic process means creating a deliberate plan that is executed over a period of time. There is no "What do we need to do today?" or "How should we tackle this next month?" Authority Marketing requires a carefully defined blueprint that is implemented methodically over time because, as I said before, no authority is gained immediately by random chance and without deliberate intention.

Next is "systematic positioning." Part-and-parcel of strategic process, "systematic positioning" means implementing your plan in such a way that it provides the most effective return on investment possible. If you're a landscaping company in Cleveland, Ohio, you're not going to try to get on the main cable news networks in Minneapolis or Pittsburgh. You're not going to pitch news stories to the *Detroit Free Press*. Rather, you focus your efforts in your business's prime radius, and you work to ensure that you are known in *every* aspect of that area's media channels. You don't just want people to recognize your company's name, you want them to see or hear your name and say, "Hey, I've been hearing a lot about those guys."

Finally, the last key term is to "command outsize influence over all competitors." This is where your unfair advantages come into play. You must position your authority so that when people think of your industry, the first name that comes to mind is you and your business. If prospects trust you more than the other guys, you win the business. If prospects think you know more than the other guys or your company is the expert over the other guys, you win the business.

At the end of the day, when you're competing in a marketplace, an industry, and a community, it's all about the sway that you have over and above other businesses to influence prospects toward your product or services.

Entrepreneur Ben Compaine once said, "The marketplace is not a podium in a quiet lecture hall, where everyone gets a turn to speak. It's more like a crowded bazaar in Casablanca. You must distract people from their main occupation—living—and show them that they can't live a minute longer without one of your beautiful rugs."

When you and your business are the authority, you have a powerful microphone and platform in that crowded bazaar, which makes all the difference.

Authority Marketing, then, is a very systematic, very deliberate plan to position yourself and your company as the expert that people want to do business with, and it's all about becoming a magnet that's attracting prospects to you, versus you having to forcefully sell.

THE JIM ZEIGLER RULE

Authority Marketing is also about fame. For any of you who are deterred by the idea of seeking fame, let me offer you one piece of advice: this isn't about ego.

Fame, when it comes to Authority Marketing, is not about you: it's about your name as a brand, your name as an authority, and your potential clients' perception that you and your business are who they want to give money to. It's about being famous where you need to be famous because people have an irrational reaction to celebrity. When you're well-known, people and potential clients not only tend to trust you, but they also flock to you. I go into this a little more in Chapter 4, and Dan touched on this irrational reaction to stardom in the foreword to this book, but in sum, if people were rational, they wouldn't rely on John Madden's advice when considering athlete's foot treatments, or they would carefully pick their face care product instead of going with Adam Levine and Sarah Michelle Gellar's recommendation to use Proactiv.

It's about fame, which is something that the figurehead of any company needs to accept if they're going to hypergrow their business, but it's not about being famous on a movie star kind of level. It's about being famous where it matters: in your marketplace, in your industry, and in your community.

Let me tell you a quick story. We have an author at Advantage by the name of Jim Zeigler. He is a consultant to automobile dealers, and he said something to me years ago that has stuck with me ever since.

"Adam," he said, "outside of the car business, nobody knows who I am. But inside the car business, I'm a friggin' rock star."

Being known and respected by people that aren't in your industry, marketplace, or community doesn't matter. They aren't the ones who are going to give you money. It doesn't matter to Jim if someone in the sports casting industry or the financial advisory business knows him from a stick in the road, because those people would never need his services.

When building your own authority, you don't need to be a worldwide celebrity. You *do* need to be *the* authority in your industry, in your community, and in the marketplace where you and your business live because you need people who have the ability and willingness to give you money and to see you as *the* authority. You need to be famous, slightly.

ROCK STARS OF AUTHORITY MARKETING

Let me give you three very different examples of people who have very successfully used Authority Marketing to their advantage. I'll start with arguably the most famous of the three . . . unless you live in Aberdeen, South Dakota, that is:

DONALD TRUMP

Donald Trump is a billionaire, which some people may say is an automatic "in" on celebrity, but just having a high income doesn't necessarily make you famous. There are four hundred names on the *Forbes* list of richest Americans, and I guarantee you that you haven't heard of 380 of them. You may have heard of the companies but not the CEOs.

So why is Trump—who actually has a lot less money than some others on that *Forbes* list—known to pretty much everyone in America?

Because he deliberately set out to develop his personal brand, build his name, and establish his authority. What he realized is that if he attached his name to real estate and his name was famous, then his real estate would instantly become more valuable, which was more equity in his pocket.

As of this book's publication date, Trump has authored fifteen books. Most billionaires have never written a book. It's not that Trump knows fifteen times more than any other billionaire; it's just that he deliberately used books to better position himself as an expert. Remember, the first six letters in authority spell "author."

He then took up the art of publicity, which to Trump meant doing outlandish things like getting into the casino business and starring on NBC's *The Apprentice*. Trump has probably lost more money from the casinos than from any other real estate deal he's ever done, but they've given him publicity, and being on *The Apprentice* meant national media attention on a weekly basis. All of these helped his fame grow even faster, and now his name is widely recognized.

I'll give you a quick, real-life example of how this Authority Marketing has directly impacted his real estate business.

In Sunny Isles Beach, Florida, there is a Trump Tower condominium building right next to two other condo complexes that are just as big, maybe bigger, and definitely just as nice as the Trump Tower. Right now, units in the Trump Tower are selling at a 30 to 40 percent premium over those two other condominium towers.

That's the power of Authority Marketing.

SUZE ORMAN

If you're in the financial services industry, forget for just a minute any opinion you may have about Suze Orman because the fact of the matter is that, as a financial advisor, she's "made it."

Ten years ago, Suze was just another small fish in a sea of 160,000 other financial advisors trying to make their way in a fiercely competitive industry.

She was doing speaking engagements and participating in programs in her community, but she was doing little else to make herself stand out from the crowd.

Then she self-published a book, and she promoted that book hard. That book led to some media appearances that gradually grew to appearances on national television and radio shows, and because she was able to portray herself as calm and personable, people saw her and felt like she was speaking the truth; they felt like they could trust her.

Suze was able to take all those little pieces of success and build them into more success so that, now, Suze isn't a financial advisor anymore. She's a media personality who's authored at least ten books and several multimedia kits on everything from wills and trusts to identity theft. She has a weekly television show on CNBC, and she speaks all over the country.

DR. DAROLD OPP

I mentioned Aberdeen, South Dakota, earlier because to many Aberdeen residents, Dr. Darold 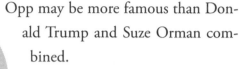 Opp may be more famous than Donald Trump and Suze Orman combined.

In Aberdeen, which is pretty much surrounded by cornfields for hundreds of miles in every direction, Dr. Opp is the most well-known dentist in his community because he's positioned himself through giving back to the community. Apart from his dentistry, he's a licensed lay pastor to eight churches in his area, including his own; he works with charitable outreach programs; he teaches an entrepreneur class at the University of Nebraska; and he's the founder of the town's annual SmilePalooza festival, which attracts thousands of kids in the region every year.

People in Aberdeen love him and want to see him. Kids actually look forward to going to the dentist because they want to see Dr. Opp. He's slightly famous within his community, and while people outside of Aberdeen may not know who he is, that doesn't matter. They're not the ones who are going to give him money, so being famous to them isn't what's important.

Effective Authority Marketing doesn't require that you become wildly famous, like a Trump; just slightly famous, like Dr. Opp. If you choose to do so—if you continue to strategically plan and systematically position yourself beyond your slight celebrity status—you could gain authority beyond your defined audience to a statewide or even nationwide authority.

But ask someone like Dr. Opp how being slightly famous is treating him, and he'll probably tell you that he already has far more business than he can handle—which is a problem we're all aiming to have.

CHAPTER 4

FOUR REASONS FOR AUTHORITY MARKETING

Dan Kennedy, the author of this book's foreword and known direct marketing expert, has been using Authority Marketing for the better part of his forty-year professional career, and over that time he's developed what he likes to call "The Four Reasons for Authority Marketing." These are:

1. Be known where you live.

2. Be the one everyone wants to go to for a high-value product or service.

3. Be the person whom others of influence want to stand next to.

4. Leverage your authority for autonomy.

These four reasons are the goals that any businessperson looking to hypergrow his or her business should have.

Paul McCartney once commented that he and John Lennon used to say to each other, "Now, let's write a swimming pool."

They said this because they had earned such a level of authority as singer/songwriters that they could sit down, put pen to paper, and shortly thereafter have sold whatever ditty they worked up for at least the cost of a new swimming pool.

That ability to have income at will is the power of Authority Marketing.

Is your business to the point where you could sit down and write a swimming pool? If not, then it's time to learn how to develop these four essential factors so that you can push your business up, over, and rocket past your current revenue plateau and into some serious hypergrowth.

REASON #1: BE KNOWN WHERE YOU LIVE

Being known where you live doesn't always mean geographically. It means achieving familiarity and recognition where your clients live—whether that's within a tri-state area or in a specific professional field.

In essence, this first reason for Authority Marketing is what Jim Zeigler meant when he said that, "Outside of the car business, nobody knows who I am. But inside of the car business, I'm a friggin' rock star."

For Jim, all that mattered to him was that others in the car industry knew who he was and purposefully pursued him for his services.

For our dentist friend Dr. Opp, the vast majority of his clientele are from Aberdeen, South Dakota, so why care about being known beyond that point?

If you're a dentist in Aberdeen, you don't need to be famous in California. You don't even need to be famous in the South Dakota capital city of Pierre. If your clients are located nationally or internationally, you don't need to be known to everyone, only to your target audience who has the capacity to do business with you. Pursuing fame for any wider an audience is a fool's errand and is only done for the sake of ego.

REASON #2: BE THE ONE EVERYONE WANTS TO GO TO

In a field of sameness, you need to be the person or company that people prefer to go to. The key to this second reason relates back to the first reason for Authority Marketing—you want to be the one whom everyone wants to go to for your product or service, but you don't necessarily need to be known by those who wouldn't use your services or products. You need to be known as *the* authority in your specific community, industry, and marketplace, whether that's on an international basis in a specific field, such as the best financial management software for the world's top one percent of paint manufacturers, or on a hometown level if your business is geographically defined, like Dr. Opp's. You need to be known only on the levels and in the fields where your customers exist.

And that's really the big idea. This is why it's so important to be slightly famous. You could spend gobs of money trying to be well-known in your industry across broad areas, but doing so is the same as casting that net over and over again into an opaque sea. Without a target, that tremendous effort is almost entirely wasted, and you are spending money with no ability to recoup that investment. But if you choose the right lure and focus on the places where you know your customers live, then your efforts are going to pay off.

Take Advantage author Mary Beall Adler, otherwise known as "The Bagel Lady." She's the owner of Georgetown Bagelry, a bagel shop in Washington, DC—one of dozens of bagel shops in a relatively small area. Over the years, she was able to grow her business to the point of making more than four hundred dozen bagels per day, but her business had more or less plateaued. Then, a couple years back, she published the book *Who Scooped My Bagel?*, and shortly after the launch of a significant marketing campaign, her business leapt another 10 percent, which for any established business is near impossible to achieve.

Georgetown Bagelry is now famous in Washington, DC—members of Congress eat there regularly, and teenagers at the local private school line up every morning for The Bagel Lady's famous bacon, egg, and cheese bagels—but outside of D.C., her shop is practically unknown.

But why should it be known beyond her customer base? It doesn't need to be, because those people aren't her potential customers. Where Mary lives, she's made Georgetown Bagelry a celebrity in it's own right, and people go out of their way to buy from her. Local coffee shops proudly boast that they serve her bagels fresh every morning, and those teenagers who get their sandwiches from her every morning will be customers for life. And those, ultimately, are a few of the top goals of any business: to be the place that people go out of their way to visit, that people commit themselves to, and where others brag that they're associated with you.

REASON #3: BE THE PERSON WHOM OTHERS OF INFLUENCE WANT TO STAND NEXT TO

This leads us to the third reason for Authority Marketing. By making yourself and your business known in your marketplace, in your community, and in your industry, people will want to associate with you. They will want to brag about being associated with you, and consequently, people of greater and greater notoriety will want to be seen with you.

This becomes a self-perpetuating cycle. The more people of notoriety who are seen with you, the more well known you become and the more people of increasingly greater influence want to be seen with you, which leads to more visibility with the general public and the resulting subconscious association that, "Well, if such-and-such likes them, then they must be good."

I'll give you a micro example from my own experience. I'm an entrepreneur in Charleston, South Carolina, which despite its recent popularity is still a relatively small city. In 2015, we had an election for mayor—the first mayoral election without our incumbent and much-beloved Mayor Joe Riley in forty years. Six people ran for his seat that year and out of those six, four approached me personally and requested a meeting to gain my support. Why?

Because I'm a young entrepreneur with a fast-growing company headquartered down-town. Because I've been featured as one of Inc. magazine's top 30 Under 30, and my company has been on the *Inc.* 500/5,000 list for the last three years. I'm the author of seven books, and I've created a reputation and brand for myself and Advantage Media Group, and those are all things that politicians want to associate with.

You may say that having politicians care about standing next to you doesn't really matter because they're not the ones giving you money and, in fact, they probably want *your* money, but that's not really the point. The point is that this kind of attention is a sign that other people of influence are attracted to you and that you're well respected within the community. It's illustrative of the fact that you're growing your standing within your niche and that others, seeing this, will also want to be a part of what you are doing.

When you attract the right people to yourself and your business, you bring more deals in, and that's the goal.

REASON #4: LEVERAGE YOUR AUTHORITY FOR AUTONOMY

With these three factors in play—people knowing who you are, people going out of their way to do business with you, and people of influence standing next to you and increasing your visibility, notoriety, and appeal—then you are able to achieve the ultimate fourth reason for Authority Marketing: leveraging your authority for autonomy.

The more of an authority figure you are in your industry, marketplace, and community, the more negotiating power you have and the higher the fees you can command without people balking or comparing you to others. And that, at the end of the day, is what it's really all about. It's the reason we're entrepreneurs.

How do you build an Authority Marketing plan? The process is different for everyone, but everyone who is successful at it aims to hit a minimum of seven main focus areas, which we'll call the Seven Pillars of Authority Marketing.

CHAPTER 5

THE SEVEN PILLARS OF AUTHORITY MARKETING

There are many ways to build an effective Authority Marketing plan beyond these focus areas, but if you're going to put the time and effort into developing your authority and developing it properly, you'll need to have a solid presence in each of the following Seven Pillars:

PILLARS OF AUTHORITY MARKETING

- BRANDING & OMNIPRESENCE
- REFERRAL MARKETING
- CONTENT MARKETING
- LEAD GENERATION
- PR & MEDIA
- SPEAKING
- EVENTS

1. BRANDING & OMNIPRESENCE

Most people know what brand is. You have a logo, you have a color scheme, you may even have a motto. But that's for your business. What about you? What's your personal brand? If I typed your-name-dot-com into my site search bar, what would come up? Would it be a website about you listing your achievements, recent awards, charitable outreach, and the books you've written, or would it lead me to a completely unrelated site about squirrel feeders or, maybe worse, nothing at all?

Building brand isn't just about building your company's brand but also your personal brand. And you not only need to do those part-and-parcel with each other, but you also need to do so universally. In order for your audience to recall your name, it must be clearly recognizable and associated in their mind. For an individual, this includes character traits such as integrity and charisma, as well as your skills and earned credentials.

Before you can create visual images, logos, and on-line copy to showcase who you are, you must distill your personal brand into what makes you unique. This will be different for everyone, but a few key factors will help you discover your brand. Consider how your *personal mission* may separate you from the masses, like "Help ten thousand people get clean water" or "Eliminating bad hires." Your *philosophy* or approach to life may differentiate you, like the socially responsible TOMS shoes founder, Blake Mycoskie, who donates a pair of shoes to someone in need every time a pair is sold. Your *journey* may be the most memorable aspect of your brand, especially if you overcame a great obstacle to become successful. Many experts focus on their teachings or *science*—the insight and knowledge that only you have in your industry. Finally, your *tribe* or community may be a highlight of your personal brand. If you led the championship football team or served on the American Bar Association, then you have personal brand qualities as a leader of a group.

Well-known leaders are very clear about who they are and what image they convey to their audience. They work hard to reinforce their best qualities in every communication about them, whether it is a radio interview, an article quote, or their online profiles.

2. CONTENT MARKETING

Content marketing is how you build that omnipresence. You and/or your team need to be committed to creating a significant amount of high-quality content written specifically for your target audience. This content can come in multiple forms. Most significantly, of course, is authorship of a book, but there are also whitepapers, special reports, articles, blog posts, webinars, teleseminars, and podcasts, to name a few. The focus should be on creating rich content for social media and constantly sharing valuable information with your target audiences. As you create appreciable content, you also create a legion of fans that are excited to consume what you create.

The content you create serves a specific purpose: to educate your prospects and customers. Your content should build trust and credibility, so it is very important that your statements are accurate and helpful. Each piece you create should help your prospect answer a question or learn more about how to use your services. Savvy content marketers create sequences of content, strategically linked from one topic to the next, to stimulate the reader to engage more. The more engaged your audience is, the more likely you are to convert them to a paying customer.

Of course, you may know your stuff and can write tons of content about what you do, but is it content your audience wants to read? One mistake many entrepreneurs make is writing advanced articles about their topic when their customer is still in the initial stages of research and needs a 101 lesson. To be an authority, you must know your topic inside and out and be able to translate it into the right language that will resonate with your audience.

Finally, there is timing. You must be consistent with your content or it loses its effectiveness. You don't want them to forget you! Content marketing is about being top of mind when your prospect is ready to buy, so you need regular, well-timed content. If there is a new trend or recent news story that affects your industry, get your perspective out to your audience before someone else does. Be their go-to source for great information, and they will return to you for advice as the true thought leader in the industry.

3. PR & MEDIA

Getting your name and your company's name mentioned in media is important because most people don't believe what you say about yourself, but they'll believe what others have to say about you. More importantly, they believe what major media has to say about you. The authority that comes when you're featured or interviewed on radio, TV, magazines, or newspapers is significant because it helps with omnipresence. Additionally, having all of these mentions across multiple media platforms also helps to build your online presence or what's known as your "digital footprint."

If I Googled your name, for instance, would I have to pack a lunch?

Think about that for a second. What I mean is, would it take me so much time to go through all of the results that come up that I could eat lunch while doing it? If the answer is no, then you have an Authority Marketing problem that needs to be solved.

In the age of commerce that we live in, Google is a vehicle for decision making. If your presence online doesn't dominate the competition, then you lose. This is why content marketing and branding are so valuable. They see your company mentioned in media, they visibly associate with the logo, and when they search for you online, they find a bevy of information, including other media outlets mentioning you.

The fact of the matter is that the mass public trusts the mainstream media. Whether you appear on CNBC or on a local radio station, people will assume that you're an authority because why else would these outlets invite you on as a guest? It's irrational, but again, there's nothing rational about the general public's decision-making process.

Marketing is about perception and, hopefully, that perception is built on reality. But people buy the perception, not the reality, and as you build your authority, the perception is that you are the number-one go-to person in your field.

4. SPEAKING

Are you currently speaking to groups that consist of your target audience? If not, and if you're uncomfortable with speaking with at least some regularity, you need to find someone else in your company with whom you're comfortable putting into a position of authority. Because speaking, bar none, is the best way to enforce your authority position and generate high-quality leads.

As a speaker, people automatically assume you're an expert or they—the company or organization putting on the seminar—wouldn't have invited you to speak. Secondly, if what you say is competent, polished, and professional, you will connect with a subset of the audience as though you were lovers at first sight. They'll want to speak with you afterward and do business with you. I can tell you from personal experience that there are at least two or three people waiting in line to talk with me after every speech I make, and all of them want to know how we can do business.

5. LEAD GENERATION

Some of you may be asking, "What does Authority Marketing have to do with lead generation?" Everything, in fact, because it's far easier to generate leads when you're seen as an authority. Back to one of the points Dan made in the foreword to this book: Are you still selling or are you able to prescribe? As an authority, you can tell people what they need, and they'll do it. But if you come at them looking and acting like a salesperson, they'll ditch you faster than a toupee in a windstorm.

The easiest way to generate high-quality leads is to have something that the leads want, including information that they find valuable. Whether you do this in the form of a book or through consistent blogging, podcasts, webinars, or any of the other various forms of direct-to-consumer marketing, the goal is to get in front of as many prospective clients as possible. This leads to omnipresence, which leads to authority.

6. REFERRAL MARKETING

How do you stimulate and encourage your satisfied clients and customers to refer you to others? It's a tricky and delicate question that most companies screw up.

What would you say if I asked you, "If your best customers went to a cocktail party, would they brag about you to their friends?"

That's another one of the main goals of Authority Marketing: to build a persona with you and your company so that clients brag to friends that they had a chance to work with you.

Referral marketing falls into two types: client referrals and referrals from influencers.

Client referrals are the most common and are an outcome of great services. Hosting a client appreciation party is a best practice used by authority marketers who want to thank their best customers and ask them for an introduction to their friends and family.

An often-missed opportunity is the referrals from influencers—more specifically, creating a target list of people who are in front of a group of your prospects every day. For a wealth management advisor, this may be a lawyer or a CPA. Once you've identified the influencers who have the ability to refer their clients to you, you must make it overly simple for them to refer. Have you ever gotten a letter in the mail from a charity with a self-addressed stamped envelope inside for you to mail back your donation? It's the same principle.

Most people want to donate or refer a client to you, but they get busy in the everyday. Make it easy for your influencers by giving them the tools they need to refer you. Tools may include a script for how to talk about you and your services, a brochure or whitepaper about what you do, a published book, or a specific landing page to learn more. Most important is to educate your influencers on when to refer you, citing key issues or concerns they might hear that your product or services address.

For both client and influencer referrals, it must be a systematic, turnkey process. Authority marketers know how many referrals they receive each year and set goals to grow this number every year by investing in those relationships and thanking the referrer.

Referral marketing is relationship marketing at its best.

7. EVENTS

Before I talk about events, let me start by saying that companies are most successful when they have loyal tribes of customers, which can be created, in great part, through effective content marketing.

Take the most obvious example: Apple. People stand in line and camp out overnight or even over a week to be the first one to buy the newest Apple product. When was the last time you saw someone camping out to get the latest edition of Windows?

Southwest flyers are fanatical about their airline, but when was the last time you saw someone fanatical about Delta? Or Nordstrom—people will go out of their way to shop there. When was the last time you saw that kind of dedication for shopping at Saks Fifth Avenue?

The most successful businesses have tribes of customers, and they create these tribes because they build relationships by *engaging their clients to the highest level possible*. This is important because engagement signifies loyalty, and loyalty signifies consumption of your product or service.

Events, then, are where these loyal tribes can come together. Salesforce.com, for example, puts on an annual event called Dreamforce that, in 2014, brought in a record 140,000 attendees from all over the world.

Holding annual events is one of the best ways to upsell, build additional loyalty, and expose more people to your tribe, making it a contagious and positive force for good.

Those, in a nutshell, are the Seven Pillars, and you can see how each relates back to the other. Every aspect feeds into the next, and all of it comes together to create a mass of positive marketing that, when implemented well and deliberately over time, leads to the ongoing and growing generation of authority and ultimately, an influx of business that allows you to do business on your own terms and only with those that you want to work with.

CHAPTER 6

AUTHORITY
BY DESIGN

How do you implement Authority Marketing for both yourself and your business? In Chapter 3, I defined Authority Marketing as the **strategic process** of **systematically positioning** a person or an organization as the leader and expert in their industry, community, and marketplace **to command outsize influence over all competitors**.

Advantage author Dr. Steven Hotze is an excellent example of Authority Marketing in action. While every entrepreneur and CEO has his or her own way of approaching Authority Marketing, I'll share here briefly how Dr. Hotze created an Authority Marketing strategy that has propelled him to authority status in his field.

DEVELOP YOUR STRATEGIC PROCESS

Today, Dr. Steven Hotze has a medical clinic in Houston, Texas, that specializes in hormones, bio-identical hormone replacement therapy, hypothyroidism, and the many other hormone issues experienced by his target market, which is mainly females in their forties and fifties.

It wasn't always this way, however. Ten years ago, Dr. Hotze had a normal medical practice. Over the course of the past decade, Dr. Hotze created and followed a deliberate Authority Marketing strategy.

He started with writing the book *Hormones, Health, and Happiness,* which directly addressed his target market and allowed him to narrow his business's focus down to a specific field of expertise, which addresses reason two: be the person that others want to go to for a specific high-value service or product.

This also allowed Dr. Hotze to begin to address two of the seven pillars: branding and omnipresence and content marketing.

Then Dr. Hotze threw in a game-changer. He got Suzanne Somers, who is very big into natural medicine and bio-identical hormone replacement therapy, to not only write a chapter in his book but also to promote and endorse it. She appreciated his services so much, in fact, that she highlighted Dr. Hotze in one of her own books.

This is the embodiment of the referral marketing pillar, as well as another excellent way to gain omnipresence. It's also reason three: he became someone whom others of influence wanted to stand next to.

SYSTEMATICALLY POSITION YOURSELF

Suzanne Somer's fame somewhat rubbed off on Dr. Hotze due to his association with her, so he leveraged that authority to systematically position himself and his book with the help of a publicist.

He started getting on radio and television shows where he talked about hypothyroidism, hormones, and other aspects of his newly re-defined practice. He wasn't on *Oprah*, but he was on *Good Day Houston, Good Morning Texas,* and KLA TV, which is the NBC station in Houston. He was also on Houston's local ABC station, Fox station, and CBS station.

He was profiled in the *Houston Chronicle* and wound end up speaking on twenty-four different radio stations in Houston, Dallas, and San Antonio.

He also placed a full-page ad in Southwest Airline's magazine, *Spirit*, since Houston is one of its hubs, and most people in Houston fly Southwest.

He didn't care about being famous to people in New Orleans or Seattle. Most of his patients were either in Houston or within a hundred miles of the city, so he concentrated all of his publicity in that area. Later, he started his own weekly radio show, launched a quarterly health magazine called *H*, and he now hosts two annual events every year for his clients, whom he refers to as "guests."

That's a full-on attack using the PR and media pillar, as well as the content marketing and events pillars. It also achieves reason one: be famous where you live.

Next, Dr. Hotze turned his focus to booking speaking engagements. He initially spoke for free to medical groups, simply asking them to buy a copy of his book at cost for every member of the audience in lieu of payment.

Why at cost? Because every time he spoke, he sent out a press release announcing that "Dr. Steven Hotze has been invited to speak at such-and-such event," and a picture of him speaking at said event would go up on his website. After the speaking engagement, every member of that audience would go home with a copy of his book, and from then on, it would be there, sitting on their nightstand or coffee table or in their living room.

That's instant lead generation, as well as a solid approach to the speaking pillar—with a little content marketing and branding and omnipresence sprinkled in.

COMMAND OUTSIZE INFLUENCE OVER ALL COMPETITORS

With a firm foothold in the Houston area, Dr. Hotze made yet another move to blast out of the water any remaining competition he might have.

Beyond the desire for an expert in his particular field, Dr. Hotze understood that his target clientele were also looking for a comfortable, if not catered-to, experience when it comes to elective medical treatments. So he chose to create a Ritz Carlton-like experience at his office and submitted articles about that experience to trade journals and newspapers in Texas.

A few of those publications bit and actually wrote stories on the experiences of real clients, including the exceptional treatment they received.

With those moves, Dr. Hotze firmly made a combined hit on the pillars of referral marketing, lead generation, content marketing, PR and media, and branding and omnipresence.

Today, he's built his definition of reason four: leveraging authority for autonomy. His medical practice is cash only—no dealing with insurance or banks or credit companies—and he has patients coming to him from twenty-two different states.

His revenues are roughly thirteen times the annual revenue of a standard private medical practice, and he's doing it all with only two full-time doctors.

Dr. Hotze didn't become famous in his field and famous in his community overnight. It took ten years of strategically positioned steps to slowly, deliberately raise his profile. But today, he commands the business and income he wants, and he's immensely happy doing it.

How do you become a Dr. Hotze? How do you become slightly famous?

You build an Authority Marketing plan, something we actually call an Authority Marketing blueprint, utilizing the Seven Pillars mentioned in this book. You then launch your plan and systematically implement that plan over time to build your authority. This is what we do day in and day out for professionals around the globe who are now authorities and leaders of their field.

I hope this book has left you enlightened and encouraged to deliberately use Authority Marketing to grow your own business and position yourself as an expert and leader in your industry. Reading this was the first step. Whether you take the next steps depends on how much you truly want to succeed.

Are you ready to take the first step to becoming an authority and leading your field?

ABOUT THE AUTHOR

Adam Witty is the founder and CEO of Advantage, The Business Growth Company. Advantage is the Authority Marketing company for entrepreneurs, business leaders, and professionals. Advantage offers turnkey publishing and marketing systems to position individuals and brands as leaders in their field. Advantage Members hail from forty US states and thirteen countries.

Adam was named to the prestigious *Inc.* 30 Under 30 list of America's Coolest Entrepreneurs in 2011. Advantage has been named to the *Inc.* 500/5000 list and the South Carolina Best Places to Work list for the past three years. Adam is the author of five books and has appeared in *USA Today, Investors Business Daily, Wall Street Journal*, and on ABC and FOX. Adam's most recent book, *Book the Business: How to Make Big Money with Your Book without Even Selling a Single Copy,* was coauthored with marketing legend Dan Kennedy.

Adam is the chairman of the Authority Marketing Institute, which is the place for the best information, teachings, and strategies on the topic. He is the publisher of *Authority Marketing Magazine* and *Advantage Magazine*. Adam is also the host of the annual Authority Marketing Summit, the largest conference held each year on Authority Marketing.

Adam loves to hear from readers. To connect:

Adam Witty
c/o Advantage Media Group
65 Gadsden Street
Charleston, SC 29401
awitty@advantageww.com
1.866.755.1696